Icy Seas

Kimberley Jane Pryor

Smart Apple Media

Smart Apple Media
2140 Howard Drive West
North Mankato, Minnesota 56003

First published in 2007 by
MACMILLAN EDUCATION AUSTRALIA PTY LTD
627 Chapel Street, South Yarra, Australia 3141

Visit our Web site at www.macmillan.com.au or go directly to www.macmillanlibrary.com.au

Associated companies and representatives throughout the world.

Copyright © Kimberley Jane Pryor 2007

Library of Congress Cataloging-in-Publication Data

Pryor, Kimberley Jane.
    Icy seas / by Kimberley Jane Pryor.
    p. cm. — (Wonders of the sea)
    Includes index.
    ISBN 978-1-59920-143-6
    1. Marine ecology—Polar regions—Juvenile literature. I. Title.

    QH95.56.P79 2007
    577.7—dc22

                                                                        2007004808

Edited by Erin Richards
Text and cover design by Christine Deering
Page layout by Domenic Lauricella
Photo research by Legend Images

Printed in U.S.

Acknowledgements
The author and the publisher are grateful to the following for permission to reproduce copyright material:

Cover photograph: Chinstrap penguins courtesy of Jeremy Colman/Lochman Transparencies.

age fotostock/Mark Jones, p. 24; Jean-Paul Ferrero/AUSCAPE, p. 16; Australian Picture Library/Minden, p. 22; Coo-ee Picture Library, p. 25; Dreamstime, pp. 3, 11, 13, 21; Mark Votier/Hulton Archive/Getty Images, p. 29; Institute of Marine Science, School of Fisheries and Ocean Sciences, University of Alaska Fairbanks, photo by Elizabeth Calvert, p. 23; Jeremy Colman/Lochman Transparencies, pp. 1, 7, 12 (bottom), 14, 19; David Stewart/Lochman Transparencies, pp. 5, 9; NASA Goddard Space Flight Center, p. 4; Jeanne Cato/National Science Foundation, p. 10; Emily Stone/National Science Foundation, p. 18; NOAA, photo by Jamie Hall, p. 27 (left); Photolibrary.com/OSF/David B. Fleetham, p. 27 (right); Photolibrary.com/OSF/Gerard Soury, p. 20; Photolibrary.com/Robert Harding Picture Library Ltd, p. 30; Photolibrary.com/British Antarctic Survey/Science Photo Library, pp. 17, 28; Photolibrary.com/Eye Of Science/Science Photo Library, p. 12 (top); Photolibrary.com/J.G. Paren/Science Photo Library, p. 15; Photolibrary.com/Andrew Syred/Science Photo Library, pp. 8, 26; Photos.com, p. 6.

While every care has been taken to trace and acknowledge copyright, the publisher tenders their apologies for any accidental infringement where copyright has proved untraceable. Where the attempt has been unsuccessful, the publisher welcomes information that would redress the situation.

For Nick, Thomas and Ashley
– Kimberley Jane Pryor

Contents

Glossary words

When a word is printed in **bold**, you can look up its meaning in the glossary on page 31.

The sea

The sea is a very large area of salty water.
It covers most of Earth's surface.

The blue part of Earth is the sea.

The sea has many different **habitats**. Icy seas are habitats that are found in the coldest parts of the world.

Large chunks of ice float in icy seas.

Icy seas

Icy seas get so cold in winter that **sea ice** forms on their surface. They are found in the **Arctic** and the **Antarctic**.

The Antarctic is ice-covered land surrounded by icy seas.

Although icy seas are very cold, they are full of life.
They provide food and shelter for many different
plants and animals.

Chinstrap penguins are found in the Antarctic.

Plants

Huge numbers of tiny plants, called plant plankton, float in the water. They are important because many sea animals depend on them for food.

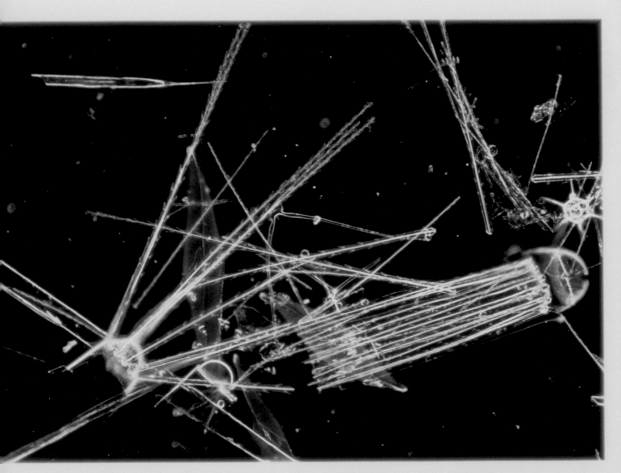

Tiny plants are found near the surface of icy seas.

Larger plants, called seaweed, grow on the **shores** of icy seas. The seaweed provides food for small animals, such as sea urchins.

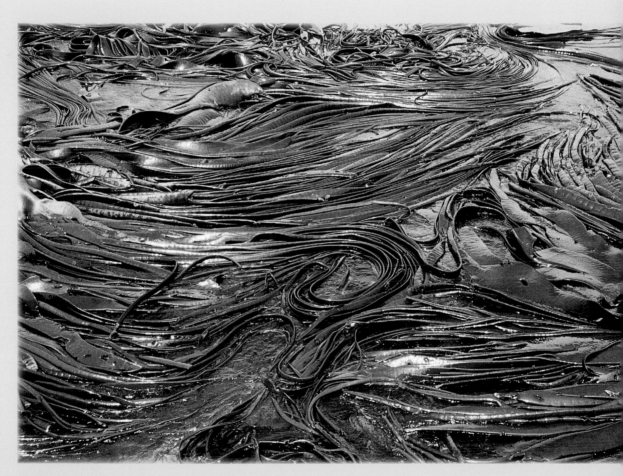

Bull kelp is a large seaweed.

Animals

Many different animals live in icy seas. Penguins, seals, and whales live in the Antarctic.

A killer whale surfaces in the Antarctic.

Walruses, seals, and polar bears live in the Arctic.
They swim in the water and rest on the sea ice.

Ringed seals often rest on sea ice.

Where animals live

In icy seas, each kind of animal has a special place to live.

Tiny animals live near the surface of the sea.

Antarctic sea stars creep along the sea floor.

Arctic puffins nest on the land, but dive underwater to catch fish.

Beluga whales swim in the icy waters of the Arctic.

Survival

To survive in icy seas, animals need to find and eat food. Penguins have long flippers and webbed feet to help them chase and catch food.

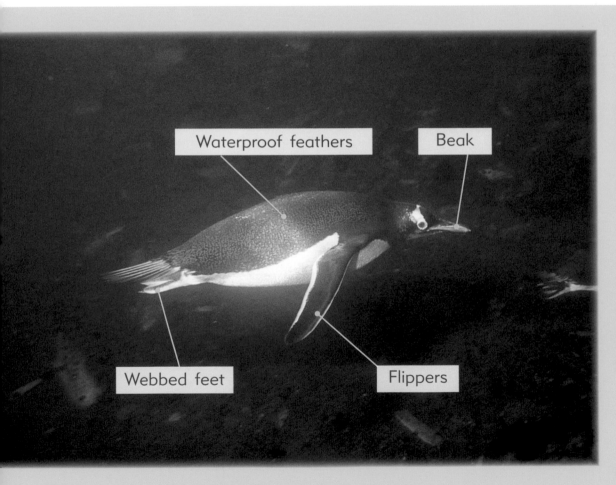

Waterproof feathers

Beak

Webbed feet

Flippers

Gentoo penguins eat krill and fish.

Animals also need to protect themselves from **predators**. Some use their colors and others use their body parts.

Crabeater seals use their flippers to swim away from predators.

Flippers for swimming

Flippers for swimming

Large eyes for seeing in deep water

Nostrils that close underwater

Small animals

Many small animals live in icy seas. Large numbers of krill live near the surface of the water.

Krill often gather in big swarms.

Squid swim around in icy seas. Sponges, corals, and sea urchins all live on the sea floor.

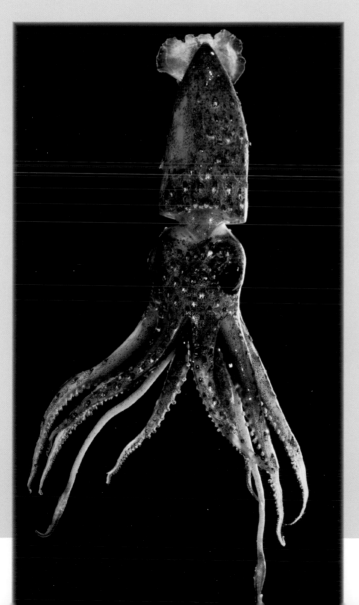

Arctic squid have long bodies to help them swim quickly.

Large animals

Large animals live in icy seas. Penguins are birds that cannot fly but can swim and dive very well.

Emperor penguins live in the Antarctic.

They can dive deeper than any other bird.

Seals are also very good swimmers and divers. They are **flexible** animals that often twist and turn as they swim.

Weddell seals swim around and under the sea ice in the Antarctic.

In the Arctic, walruses spend a lot of time in the water. They come onto the sea ice to rest.

Walruses often lie beside one another on the sea ice.

Polar bears spend most of their time on the sea ice. They can swim for long distances when hunting for seals.

Polar bears have white fur to help them blend in with the sea ice.

Fish

Fish that live in icy seas can survive in very cold water.

This Antarctic fish can survive in icy seas.

Icy sea fish have special **chemicals** in their bodies. The chemicals keep them from freezing.

The Arctic cod is found in the icy Arctic seas.

Living together

Sometimes animals live together for protection. Penguins gather together at the edge of the water. They all check for predators before diving in.

When one Adélie penguin jumps into the water, the others quickly follow.

Some animals survive by living on another kind of animal. Some barnacles attach themselves to whales. They take their food from the water as the whale swims along.

The lumps on the humpback whale are barnacles.

Food chain

Living things depend on other living things for food. This is called a food chain.

This is how a food chain works.

Plant 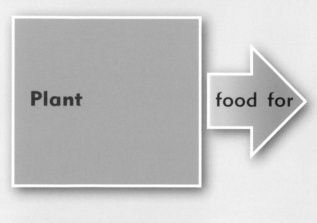 food for

This is a simple icy seas food chain.

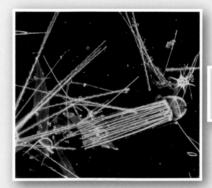 food for

Tiny plants make their food using energy from the sun.

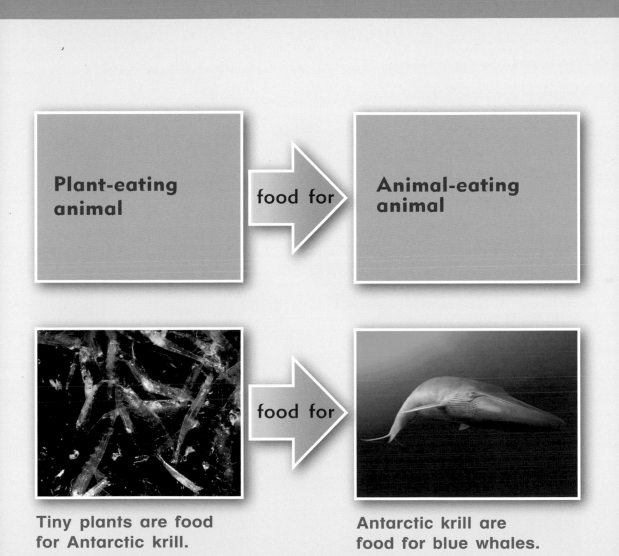

Plant-eating animal **food for** Animal-eating animal

Tiny plants are food for Antarctic krill.

Antarctic krill are food for blue whales.

Threats to icy seas

Icy seas can be **threatened** by natural events, such as very warm winters. Not as many krill survive when winters are too warm.

One Adélie penguin is feeding krill to the other.

Icy seas are also threatened by people who:

- put garbage into the sea
- catch so many animals that some are in danger of becoming **extinct**
- let boats **run aground** and spill oil

Whalers travel to the Antarctic to hunt and kill whales.

Protecting icy seas

We help protect icy seas when we:

- keep garbage on the land
- look at icy sea animals instead of hunting them
- make sure boats do not run aground

Cruise ships take tourists to look at icy seas.

Glossary

Antarctic   the area around the South Pole

Arctic   the area around the North Pole

chemicals   the substances that things are made of

extinct   no longer existing

flexible   able to bend easily

habitats   places where plants or animals naturally grow or live

predators   animals that hunt, kill, and eat other animals

run aground   when a boat hits the sea floor and gets stuck

sea ice   ice that forms on the surface of the sea

shores   land along the edges of the sea

threatened   placed in danger

Index